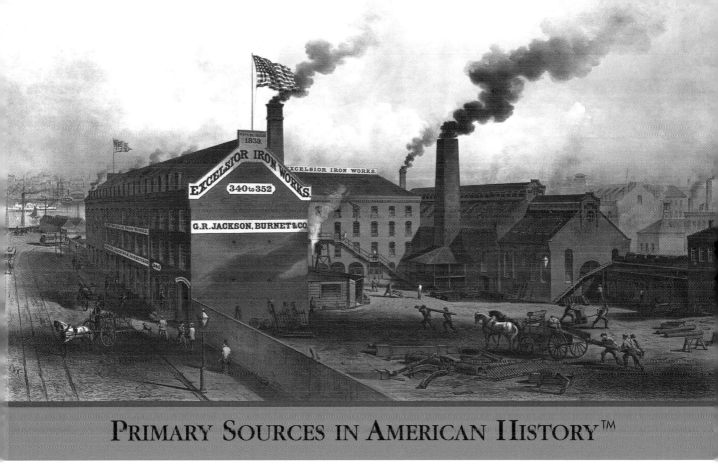

PRIMARY SOURCES IN AMERICAN HISTORY™

THE INDUSTRIAL REVOLUTION IN AMERICA

A PRIMARY SOURCE HISTORY OF AMERICA'S TRANSFORMATION INTO AN INDUSTRIAL SOCIETY

CORONA BREZINA

rosen central
Primary Source™

The Rosen Publishing Group, Inc., New York

Published in 2005 by The Rosen Publishing Group, Inc.
29 East 21st Street, New York, NY 10010

First Edition

Library of Congress Cataloging-in-Publication Data

Brezina, Corona.
The industrial revolution in America: A primary source history of America's
    transformation into an industrial society/by Corona Brezina.
        p. cm—(Primary sources in American history)
Summary: Uses primary source documents, narrative, and illustrations to recount the history of the industrial revolution in the United States, as society changed from reliance on agriculture and trade to modern manufacture. Includes bibliographical references and index.
ISBN 1-4042-0179-3 (library binding)
1. Industrial revolution—United States—Juvenile literature. 2. Industries—United States—History—Juvenile literature. 3. Technological innovations—Social aspects—United States—History—Juvenile literature. [1. Industrial revolution—United States. 2. Industries—United States—History. 3. Technological innovations. 4. United States—Economic conditions—To 1865.]
I. Title. II. Series: Primary sources in American history (New York, N.Y.)
HC105.B82 2004
330.973'05—dc22

                                                                                2003022726

Manufactured in the United States of America

On the front cover: An 1848 color lithograph of the Oswego Starch Factory in Oswego, New York.

On the back cover: First row (left to right): John Bakken's sod house in Milton, North Dakota; Oswego Starch Factory in Oswego, New York. Second row (left to right): *American Progress,* painted by John Gast in 1872; the Battle of Palo Alto. Third row (left to right): Pony Express rider pursued by Native Americans on the plains; Union soldiers investigating the rubble of a Southern building.

CONTENTS

NTRODUCTION

The Industrial Revolution, a period of rapid technological advancements, began in Britain in the mid-eighteenth century and eventually spread across the world over the next 150 years. It changed the way the world produces its goods. As a result, it transformed many countries from mostly rural agricultural societies into modern economies in which industry and manufacturing are the primary drivers of the economy.

FROM AGRICULTURE TO INDUSTRY

During the revolution, machines took on tasks that before had been done by people and animals. Innovators discovered new and more efficient ways of transforming raw materials into products that met human needs. Also, advances in transportation allowed people and goods to move cheaply and easily from one place to another.

But the Industrial Revolution also brought new social perils. At first, it swept newly out-of-work skilled artisans and small farmers into cities to work in factories, eventually replacing them with a class of unskilled labor. Entire families, including young children, were forced into the workforce as the gap between rich and poor increased. The sources of energy used to run factories have been proved to be damaging to the environment.

The transformation in the United States was particularly striking. Early Americans spent long hours farming the land and attending to household tasks. As the United States became industrialized, many people put in even longer hours laboring in factories for low wages. Working conditions were often unhealthy and hazardous. As a result, more and more people called for social and economic reforms. Workers wanted laws to limit the workweek and improve working conditions and pay. Over time, federal and state governments enacted regulations that addressed some labor concerns.

Between 1790, when the first factory was built in the country, and 1908, when Henry Ford introduced an automobile for the average American, the United States changed from a sparsely populated nation of small farmers into an urbanized, industrial society. The technological developments during this period set the stage for the United States to become the global superpower it is today.

TIMELINE

1769 —— James Watt patents an improved steam engine that can power textile mills.

1785 —— Thomas Jefferson argues against industrialization in his *Notes on Virginia*.

1790 —— Samuel Slater and his partners build the first textile mill in the United States.

1793 —— Eli Whitney invents the cotton gin.

1798 —— Whitney accepts a government contract to manufacture muskets.

1807 —— Robert Fulton travels up the Hudson River by steamboat.

1825 —— The Erie Canal is completed.

1826 —— The industrial city of Lowell, Massachusetts, is officially named for Francis Cabot Lowell.

1837 —— John Deere introduces a plow with steel blades.

1844 —— Samuel Morse sends the first long-distance telegraph message.

TIMELINE

1848 —— Cyrus McCormick opens the McCormick Reaper Works in Chicago.

1869 —— The first transcontinental railroad is completed; the Knights of Labor, a labor organization, is founded.

1876 —— Alexander Graham Bell invents the telephone.

1877 —— Thomas Edison patents the phonograph; railway workers participate in massive strikes across the country.

1879 —— Edison perfects the incandescent light bulb.

1882 —— Edison's electric light and power system begins operation in New York City.

1886 —— On May 1, strikers across the country call for an eight-hour workday. The Haymarket bombing occurs in Chicago.

1903 —— Wilbur and Orville Wright make the first manned flight in an airplane.

1908 —— Ford introduces the Model T automobile.

CHAPTER 1

INDUSTRY IN EARLY AMERICA

When the United States declared independence in 1776, it was a nation of farmers and artisans. Americans worked the land and ran businesses out of their homes or small shops. Whenever possible, they made their own furniture, tools, clothes, and other goods. Artisans, or skilled craftsmen, specialized in making goods such as shoes, watches, metalwork, and dishes. Complex items were each individually crafted. For example, a gunsmith would cast and refine each component of the gun before fitting the pieces together, so every one of his guns was unique. Families traded and sold most goods locally. Traders could not afford to transport imports and manufactured goods to isolated rural towns.

The United States possessed a wealth of natural resources, which eventually helped drive the Industrial Revolution. It had vast expanses of fertile, unsettled land and a network of waterways. Forests provided plentiful timber that colonists burned for fuel and used for building houses, furniture, ships, barrels, and much more. Rich deposits of iron ore could be worked into raw iron or, by the time of the Industrial Revolution, smelted into steel.

This circa 1850 painting, entitled *He That Tilleth the Land Shall Be Satisfied*, portrays what life was like in the United States before the Industrial Revolution. Most Americans were employed in agriculture, where the work was seasonal. Farms were hectic during periods of planting and harvest and relaxed at other times, especially in places that experienced cold winters.

Despite America's natural wealth, the Industrial Revolution did not originate in the United States. The first technological breakthroughs occurred in Britain.

British Innovations

The British Industrial Revolution began with the mechanization of the textile industry in the early eighteenth century. Production of cloth had traditionally been a cottage industry. Spinners and weavers would produce thread and cloth in their homes using spinning wheels or hand looms. The old system began to change in 1733, when John Kay invented the flying shuttle. His invention allowed weavers to work much more quickly, but spinners could no longer work fast enough to supply weavers with thread. Other inventors responded by building spinning machines. Among these was a huge spinning frame powered by water that was invented by a wig maker named Richard Arkwright in 1769. These new machines now produced too much thread for the weavers to handle. To address this problem, Edmund Cartwright built the first power loom in 1785. By the early nineteenth century, the cottage textile industry had disappeared. Instead of spinning or weaving thread and cloth in their homes, textile workers operated machines in factories.

The earliest factories were powered by water and had to be built beside rivers or streams. But inventors had already begun developing steam engines that could provide factories with power. Thomas Newcomen built the first practical steam engine in 1712. Deep shafts in coal mines often flooded, and Newcomen's invention pumped out the water.

Scottish inventor James Watt refined the steam engine in 1769, eventually producing an efficient alternative to water power. Fueled by coal, the steam engine heated water to the point of evaporation, generating steam. Watt discovered how to use steam power to turn the gears of textile mills. Industrialists across Britain adopted his steam engine in their factories. Since the steam engine was fueled by coal, coal production also increased.

Also during the eighteenth century, a series of innovations, sometimes called the "iron revolution," allowed the British to efficiently produce high-quality iron. Iron and steel would become the most important raw materials of the Industrial Revolution. Railways, industrial machinery, and buildings all required huge amounts of iron and steel.

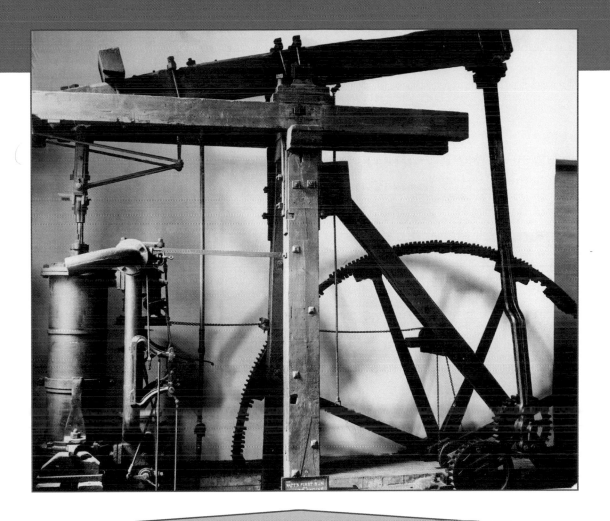

Pictured here is James Watt's first steam engine, which is housed in the Science Museum in London, England. In 1774, Watt entered into a partnership with industrialist Michael Boulton to manufacture the engines. They created approximately 500 steam engines before Watt's patent expired in 1800. Originally used to pump water from mine shafts, Watt's engines were later used in steamships.

Two Revolutions in America

The American Revolution, lasting from 1775 to 1781, coincided with the beginning of the Industrial Revolution. By 1790, all thirteen original states of the newly established United States ratified the Constitution. But the leaders of the young country still disagreed on many critical issues. Some of the Founding Fathers nervously observed the changes engulfing Britain. They feared that the Industrial Revolution would completely transform Americans' way of life if it spread to the United States. Should the government concentrate on developing America's agricultural resources or instead promote industrialization?

Thomas Jefferson, president of the United States from 1801 to 1809, wanted the United States to remain an agricultural nation. He had spent years in Europe, where "manufacture must therefore be resorted to of necessity not of choice, to support the surplus of their people," as he wrote in his book *Notes on Virginia*, published in 1785. Jefferson envisioned a nation of self-reliant "yeomen farmers" who did not depend on government or industry for goods and services. Like many Americans, Jefferson believed that industrialization and urbanization—the growth of cities—produced wretched living and working conditions. "For the general operations of manufacture, let our workshops remain in Europe," he wrote. "It is better to carry provisions and materials to workmen there, than bring them to the provisions and materials, and with them their manners and principles. The loss by the transportation of commodities across the Atlantic will be made up in happiness and permanence of government."

In 1791, Alexander Hamilton submitted his *Report on Manufactures* to Congress. It proposed that the government actively work to develop American industry. He wrote: "In countries where there is great private wealth, much may be effected by the voluntary contributions of patriotic individuals; but in a community situated like that of the United States, the public purse must supply the deficiency of private

In his *Report on Manufactures*, Alexander Hamilton recommended that the federal government subsidize manufacturing. He rejected arguments that the United States could prosper with an agricultural base and proposed that the nation ban the importation of goods that competed with American products. Hamilton, who was secretary of the Treasury in 1791, when he released the report, was also responsible for the establishment of the country's first national bank. Refer to page 55 for a partial transcription of Hamilton's report.

resource. In what can it be so useful, as in prompting and improving the efforts of industry?"

Hamilton argued that industry would free the United States from dependence on foreign goods. If industry replaced the handicraft system, American products could compete in the international market. Americans would be able to choose from a greater variety of occupations than ever before. Although the United States had a very small population, factories would bring women and children into the labor market. Eventually, the success of industry would attract immigrants who could work in factories as well as in agriculture. Population growth would create a greater demand for agricultural products and benefit the economy.

Congress did not act on Hamilton's report, but his vision for the United States eventually prevailed. In the early years of the nineteenth century, even Jefferson admitted the usefulness and necessity of some industry.

The First American Factories

While the British adopted steam engines and built factories during the mid-1800s, Americans developed little manufacturing capability beyond ironworks and small water-powered mills. These early mills relied on the same basic principles first applied in Europe during the Middle Ages. Gristmills ground grains, such as corn and wheat, into meal. Sawmills cut logs into lumber and firewood.

Britain jealously guarded its industrial technology. The new inventions boosted production of textile goods and gave the British an advantage in international trade. The British government passed laws banning the export of industrial machines and forbidding manufacturing experts from leaving the country.

Samuel Slater was born in Derbyshire, England, on June 9, 1768. An apprentice in a local textile factory, he was eventually promoted to supervisor of machinery and mill construction. Soon after he completed his apprenticeship, Slater immigrated to the United States. He was among the first of a group of immigrant British mechanics who brought new technologies to the United States in the late eighteenth century. Following the success of the Pawtucket, Rhode Island, cotton mill, Slater established a number of cotton-mill villages, based on the employment of whole families, throughout New England.

In 1787, a young Englishman named Samuel Slater read in the newspaper that Americans were offering generous rewards to textile experts who could help develop industry in America. Slater had just completed six years of apprenticeship to an important textile manufacturer. He disguised himself as a farmer and took passage to New York. In partnership with two merchants, Slater opened a water-powered spinning mill in Pawtucket, Rhode Island. He replicated the cotton carding machine and the spinning frame

This oil painting depicts Samuel Slater's cotton mill by the Blackstone River in Pawtucket, Rhode Island. By 1800, the water-powered mill employed more than 100 workers. Created by the American School around 1790, the painting is housed at the Smithsonian Institution in Washington, D.C.

he had worked on in Britain from memory. After the mill proved a success, Slater and his partners built the first textile factory in 1793 and eventually established dozens of mills and factories.

More British textile workers immigrated to the United States, bringing with them additional information on British technology. Textile factories and entire mill towns dependent on the textile industry slowly began to multiply across New England.

CHAPTER 2

The American Industrial Revolution began with the efforts of British immigrants, but Americans soon contributed important innovations to industry. American inventors looked for ways to solve problems unique to the United States, a sparsely populated farming nation. Agriculture benefited from many of their early inventions.

Eli Whitney, Inventor

Colonists in the southern United States found the soil and climate ideal for growing cotton. But the crop could not be profitable because of the large number of laborers needed to harvest clean cotton fiber.

THE SPREAD OF INDUSTRIALIZATION

It took a worker an entire day to separate a pound or two of fiber from the cotton plant's seeds.

In 1792, a young Yale graduate named Eli Whitney accepted an invitation to visit Mrs. Nathanael Greene on her Georgia plantation. In a letter to his father, as quoted in Holland Thompson's *The Age of Invention*, Whitney wrote, "There were a number of very respectable Gentlemen at Mrs. Greene's who all agreed that if a machine could be invented which would clean the cotton with

Despite owning a patent for his revolutionary cotton gin, Eli Whitney did not make a lot of money from this invention. Whitney and his business partner Phineas Miller spent many years bringing costly lawsuits against blacksmiths who duplicated his gin without paying him for his patent. Pictured here are Whitney *(inset)* and his cotton gin patent.

expedition, it would be a great thing both to the Country and to the inventor." Whitney had a natural mechanical aptitude. He came up with a device with revolving sawtooth wheels that pulled cotton fibers through slits while leaving the seeds behind. It could clean 50 pounds (22.5 kilograms) of cotton fiber in a day.

Whitney hoped that his cotton gin, patented in 1793, would make him a fortune. Yet his cotton gin was easily duplicated and other mechanics did not respect Whitney's patent. After a series of frustrating and expensive battles in court, he turned his talents to another field.

In 1798, Whitney accepted a contract from the government to manufacture 10,000 muskets in two years. In most firearms factories, a single worker crafted each gun from start to finish. Whitney proposed to simplify the process by introducing interchangeable parts. Each worker would craft or assemble specific pieces of the musket. His system was more efficient and did not require skilled craftsmen. Broken muskets could be repaired with identical premade parts.

Whitney did not finish the 10,000 muskets until 1808, but his factory later filled an order of 15,000 muskets in only two years. He is recognized today as a pioneer in mass production. The concept of interchangeable parts eventually transformed production across a range of industries.

New Ways of Farming

Whitney's cotton gin turned cotton into a moneymaking crop. Southern plantations increased their cotton production, sending mountains of cotton to textile mills. At the same time, other inventions and improvements began revolutionizing American agriculture. Early colonists cultivated their crops with hand tools, sometimes assisted by oxen or horses. The transformation of agriculture began in 1701 when a British farmer, Jethro Tull, invented a seed-planting machine called the seed drill.

Farmers growing wheat faced the same dilemma as cotton growers. The harvest was a slow, labor-intensive process. Workers cut grain by hand with a scythe or sickle. Since wheat had to be harvested within a week or two of ripening, a lack of labor limited the size of the farmer's crop.

A number of mechanics, including Cyrus McCormick, sought to develop a mechanical reaper to harvest wheat. In 1831, McCormick successfully tested his horse-drawn reaper. The market for his reaper increased as settlers began farming western land. In 1848, McCormick set up a steam-powered factory in Chicago that drew on Whitney's system of inter-changeable parts. McCormick proved to be one of the great businessmen of the century. The McCormick Reaper Works prospered. His reaper was shown in demonstrations across the country and regularly won competitions against other reapers. McCormick aggressively advertised the reaper, set up agencies in agricultural communities, and allowed buyers to pay in installment plans.

In 1837, John Deere built a plow with steel blades that would not become clogged with soil. Previously, farmers needed to stop frequently to remove clumps of soil. Many western farmers bought John Deere plows, as well as many other labor-saving machines. Threshers collected and bound fallen wheat. American manufacturers began producing seed drills. A variety of cultivators, harrows, mowers, hay rakes, and other machines came into use during the mid-nineteenth century. Farmers began experimenting with fertilizers and crop rotation.

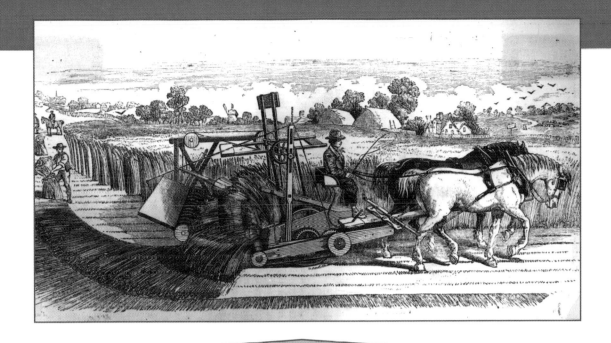

This engraving, by Burgess and Key, portrays the McCormick reaper in operation. The reaper became a favorite among farmers in the mid-nineteenth century. By 1860, Cyrus McCormick's factory in Chicago was the leading maker of farm equipment in the United States.

The Rise of the Machine

Even as agricultural innovations revolutionized farming, the expansion of industry brought dramatic changes to the lives of ordinary Americans. In 1810, the Boston, Massachusetts, merchant Francis Cabot Lowell visited Britain to study large-scale textile manufacturing. Upon his return, he worked with a small group of partners to set up a factory at Waltham, Massachusetts. Opened in 1814, the factory contained machinery to transform raw cotton into cloth all under one roof. More factories were built during the next few years, and Waltham became the first industrial city in the United States.

Lowell hired unmarried women, most between the ages of fifteen and thirty, to work in the factories. They lived in factory-owned dormitories run by matrons. Although the women worked over eleven hours each day, Lowell's system provided recreation and educational opportunities for their spare time. They were strictly supervised and were required to attend church on Sundays.

The enterprise was so successful that Lowell's partners set up an even larger factory city in 1822. They named it after Lowell, who had died in 1817. A mechanic named Paul Moody designed the machinery for this new super city. By 1835, twenty-two mills operated in Lowell. Just as in Waltham, young women worked in the factories.

Supporters of industry praised the city of Lowell's success, applauding its innovations and working conditions. According to Thomas Bender in *Toward an Urban Vision*, in a Fourth of July speech at Lowell in 1830, statesman Edward Everett compared its industrial success with "what it was ten or twelve years ago, when Lowell itself consisted of two or three quite unproductive farms. It is the contrast of production with bareness; of cultivation with waste; of plenty with an absence of every thing but the bare necessaries of life." The British writer Charles Dickens visited Lowell in 1842 and praised the town in his book *American Notes*. He was impressed by the working conditions. He wrote of the factories: "In the windows of some, there were green plants, which were trained to shade the glass; in all, there was as much fresh air, cleanliness, and comfort, as the nature of the occupation would possibly admit."

With the rise of factories and agricultural machinery, the demand increased for machine shops to make the equipment. Machine builders had to produce the engines, looms, waterworks, and much more for textile factories. As more industries became

TIME TABLE OF THE LOWELL MILLS,

Arranged to make the working time throughout the year average 11 hours per day.

TO TAKE EFFECT SEPTEMBER 21st., 1853.

The Standard time being that of the meridian of Lowell, as shown by the Regulator Clock of AMOS SANBORN, Post Office Corner, Central Street.

From March 20th to September 19th, inclusive.

COMMENCE WORK, at 6.30 A. M.   LEAVE OFF WORK, at 6.30 P. M., except on Saturday Evenings.
BREAKFAST at 6 A. M.   DINNER, at 12 M.   Commence Work, after dinner, 12.45 P. M.

From September 20th to March 19th, inclusive.

COMMENCE WORK at 7.00 A. M.   LEAVE OFF WORK, at 7.00 P. M., except on Saturday Evenings.
BREAKFAST at 6.30 A. M.   DINNER, at 12.30 P. M.   Commence Work, after dinner, 1.15 P. M.

BELLS.

From March 20th to September 19th, inclusive.

Morning Bells.	Dinner Bells.	Evening Bells.
First bell,............4.30 A. M.	Ring out,.............12.00 M.	Ring out,............6.30 P. M.
Second, 5.30 A. M.; Third, 6.20.	Ring in,.............12.35 P. M.	Except on Saturday Evenings

From September 20th to March 19th, inclusive.

Morning Bells.	Dinner Bells.	Evening Bells.
First bell...........5.00 A. M.	Ring out,...........12.30 P. M.	Ring out at...........7.00 P. M.
Second, 6.00 A. M.; Third, 6.50.	Ring in,.............1.05 P. M.	Except on Saturday Evenings.

SATURDAY EVENING BELLS.

During APRIL, MAY, JUNE, JULY, and AUGUST, Ring Out, at 6.00 P. M.
The remaining Saturday Evenings in the year, ring out as follows :

SEPTEMBER.	NOVEMBER.	JANUARY.
First Saturday, ring out 6.00 P. M.	Third Saturday ring out 4.00 P. M.	Third Saturday, ring out 4.25 P. M.
Second " " 5.45 "	Fourth " " 3.55 "	Fourth " " 4.35 "
Third " " 5.30 "		
Fourth " " 5.20 "	DECEMBER.	FEBRUARY.
	First Saturday, ring out 3.50 P. M.	First Saturday, ring out 4.45 P. M.
OCTOBER.	Second " " 3.55 "	Second " " 4.55 "
First Saturday, ring out 5.05 P. M.	Third " " 3.55 "	Third " " 5.00 "
Second " " 4.55 "	Fourth " " 4.00 "	Fourth " " 5.10 "
Third " " 4.45 "	Fifth " " 4.00 "	
Fourth " " 4.35 "		MARCH.
Fifth " " 4.25 "		First Saturday, ring out 5.25 P. M.
		Second " " 5.30 "
NOVEMBER.	JANUARY.	Third " " 5.35 "
First Saturday, ring out 4.15 P. M.	First Saturday, ring out 4.10 P. M.	Fourth " " 5.45 "
Second " - " 4.05 "	Second " " 4.15 "	

YARD GATES will be opened at the first stroke of the bells for entering or leaving the Mills.

• *SPEED GATES commence hoisting three minutes before commencing work.*

This is a timetable of the cotton textile mills in Lowell, Massachusetts. It provides an indication of how rigidly the mills' management regulated its workforce of more than 10,000 young women. As can be seen at the top of the timetable, it was "arranged to make the working time throughout the year average 11 hours per day."

mechanized, large power-driven facilities using interchangeable parts replaced artisans' shops.

Advances in Transportation

At the beginning of the nineteenth century, most American roads were little more than poorly maintained pathways. Merchants found it difficult and expensive to transport their wares. Before agricultural products and manufactured goods could compete in the world market, the United States needed to improve its transportation system.

In 1806, Congress authorized the construction of the National Road, originating in Maryland and eventually stretching to Illinois. But the government never systematically planned out a network of roads, leaving that responsibility to the states. Private companies, hoping to make a profit, constructed turnpikes that connected most major cities by 1820. Workers cleared and laid the roads by hand, usually surfacing them with packed earth, logs, or broken stone. Travelers paid tolls to build and maintain the roads.

In August 1807, engineer Robert Fulton made history with his steamboat, the *North River Steam Boat* (often called the *Clermont*), when he traveled along the Hudson River from New York City to Albany. The boat was propelled by a steam engine that turned paddle wheels in the water. Immediately after the journey, Fulton wrote to his partner that "funds and spirit are now only wanting to do the handsomest and lucrative things which has been performed for some years," as quoted by Cynthia Owen Philip in *Robert Fulton: A Biography*. Other inventors had experimented with steam-powered boats, but Fulton made the steamboat a commercial success.

This etching by Samuel Hollyer portrays the 1807 maiden voyage of Robert Fulton's steamboat *Clermont* on the Hudson River, en route to Albany, New York. The *Clermont* was powered by one of James Watt's steam engines. Fulton's successful launch of the *Clermont* marked the beginning of the steamboat era. Transportation in the United States was greatly improved and increased, especially on the coasts and along the Mississippi River.

Steamboats became common sights on American waterways. They provided cheaper and faster transportation than wagons. To make water travel more convenient, engineers connected rivers by building man-made waterways called canals. Between 1815 and 1840, the United States constructed over 3,100 miles (4,991 kilometers) of canals. The most famous project was the 363-mile-long (584 km) Erie Canal connecting Albany to Buffalo, completed in 1825. It created a continuous waterway from New York City to territory around the Great Lakes, opening up the fertile land to immigration and shipping.

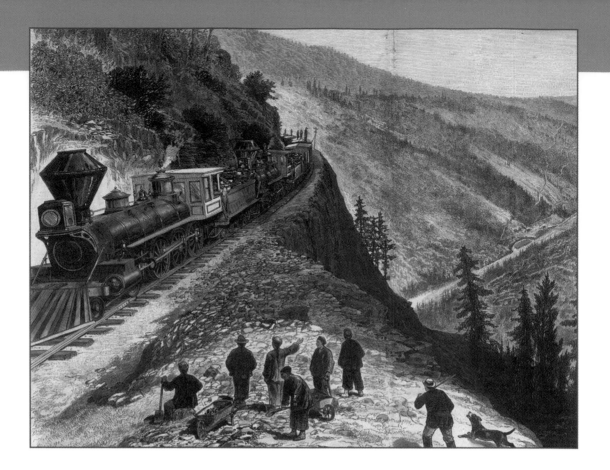

Immigrant Chinese railroad workers watch as a train rounds the bend in Coloma, California, in this engraving by Horace Baker. Between 1850 and 1882, Chinese workers were recruited as cheap laborers. They were used primarily on the West Coast to drive down wages in railroad construction, mining, and agriculture. They faced widespread discrimination.

By the 1850s, traffic on the Erie Canal had begun to decline. Travel by water was being replaced by the next revolution in transportation: railways. In the late 1820s, a few companies laid down short horse-drawn railways, usually to connect mines to canals or ports. In 1825, the British railroad and locomotive pioneer George Stephenson designed the Stockton and Darlington railway in Britain. It was the first public railway to use a steam-powered locomotive. The first American general purpose railroad, chartered in 1827, was the Baltimore and Ohio line.

The government poured money into railroad construction. By 1860, 30,000 miles (48,300 km) of railways crisscrossed the United States. Construction of tracks pushed westward, much of the grueling labor done by Irish and Chinese immigrants. In 1869, two railroads connected to form a 1,848-mile-long (2,975 km) transcontinental railway, linking the East and West Coasts.

Railroads ended regional isolation in the United States. They provided cheap transportation for industrial and agricultural products everywhere in the country. More Americans than ever before could travel long distances easily and affordably.

CHAPTER 3

In 1851, Britain held the Crystal Palace Exhibition in London. Named for its iron-and-glass exhibition building, the event was the first world's fair. Nations from across the globe showcased their artistic and technological achievements. As Americans prepared their entries, the *New York Herald* emphasized in an editorial on August 1, 1850, how much was at stake:

THE SECOND REVOLUTION

This is the first opportunity we have had of fairly laying before the world our productions of art and it should not be passed lightly by ... Now we can show them that we not only produce cotton, iron, coal, copper and gold in greater abundances than any other nation, but that we can work them up into manufactures often equally, sometimes surpassing the oldest nations in a perfection and with a facility unknown to them.

The United States entered over 500 exhibits. American agricultural manufacturers displayed plows, scythes, and other implements. The McCormick reaper won a top award and was highly praised in the London *Times*. Samuel Colt exhibited his Colt revolver. It was built using a system of interchangeable

This painting, entitled *America*, by Joseph Nash captures the grandeur of the American pavilion at the Crystal Palace Exhibition in London, England, in 1851. American products, such as the McCormick reaper, Colt revolvers, and Goodyear's vulcanized rubber were very well received. It was at this exhibition that the United States' industrial prowess was first widely recognized. The United States hosted its first international fair in New York City in 1853.

parts. Several inventors, including Elias Howe and Isaac Merrit Singer, had worked on the development of the sewing machine. Charles Goodyear won an award for his display of vulcanized rubber, a discovery he had made in 1839. The process of vulcanization made rubber more elastic and better suited to industrial uses.

The American section of the exhibit amazed everyone who attended. Britain and other industrialized countries had no idea that American technology had become so advanced. Impressed by American innovations, the British government appointed a commission to visit the United States and observe American industry. British manufacturers soon placed orders for American machines, and American goods entered the European market. The Crystal Palace Exhibition marked the beginning of the United States' rise to industrial dominance.

After the Civil War (1861–1865), industrial growth in the United States skyrocketed. Some historians call the period of technical innovations following the Civil War the Second Industrial Revolution. By the beginning of the twentieth century, manufacturing had surpassed agriculture in the economy. Cities swelled as workers moved from farms to factories. Large corporations came to dominate industries, replacing small local businesses. A few Americans grew fabulously wealthy, while others could barely earn a living working long hours in dangerous working conditions.

Electricity replaced steam as the most important source of power. After Edwin Drake struck oil in Pennsylvania and sank the first oil well in 1859, oil production boomed. Oil began to compete with coal as a source of fuel. Transportation and communication networks reached every corner of the country. Specialized scientists and engineers, rather than mechanics and artisans, made the major discoveries during this age. Inventors began focusing on the applications of scientific research.

In 1856, Sir Henry Bessemer of Britain discovered a method of cheaply manufacturing steel from iron. Stronger and easier to work than iron, steel became essential for constructing buildings, bridges, and railroad tracks. The first modern skyscraper, built using steel girders, was completed in Chicago, Illinois, in 1885.

AMERICAN SCENERY.

AMERICAN SCENERY.

2759. GASSING WELLS.

This photograph shows the derricks, or towers, over the United States' first oil well near Titusville, Pennsylvania. Throughout the late nineteenth century, the United States was the world's leading oil producer, refiner, consumer, and exporter. By 1880, John D. Rockefeller's Standard Oil Company controlled about 90 percent of the petroleum industry. In 1911, the Supreme Court broke Rockefeller's monopoly into thirty-four smaller companies.

Breakthroughs in Communication

In 1832, while returning home by ship from his studies in France, American inventor and artist Samuel Morse overheard his fellow passengers talking. They were discussing the French physicist André-Marie Ampère's recent experiments in electromagnetism. The revelation hit Morse that an electric current could be used to transmit messages over long distances.

Upon returning to the United States, Morse began experimenting with wires and magnets. He drew upon the research of other experts in electricity and the assistance of his colleagues Leonard Gale and Alfred Vail. Morse's work resulted in the invention of the telegraph. His invention transmitted a message across telegraph lines in bursts of electric current. An electromagnet in the receiver recorded the message as a sequence of dots and dashes, which an operator would translate back into the original message. His telegraph system of replacing letters of the alphabet with patterns of dots and dashes is known as Morse code.

In 1843, Congress granted Morse $30,000 to build an experimental telegraph line. It spanned 40 miles (64 km) between Washington, D.C., and Baltimore, Maryland. On May 1, 1844, Morse sent the first successful long-distance telegraph message, the famous phrase, "What hath God wrought?" In its first practical use the next day, Morse informed Congress that James Polk had been nominated for president by the Democratic Convention meeting in Baltimore.

Before Morse's plan of instant communication could become a reality to most Americans, telegraph lines and stations had to be constructed. Telegraph companies were quickly established and telegraph lines began to extend across the country, usually following the same paths as railways. By 1861, 23,000 miles (37,015 km) of telegraph lines spanned the United States. The next great advance in communications occurred in 1876 with Alexander Graham Bell's invention of the telephone. Bell worked as a teacher of the deaf and tinkered with inventions in his spare time. He was an expert in acoustics and the physics behind human speech. In 1872, Bell began working on the "musical telegraph," which could send different pitches across a single telegraph wire. His focus changed in 1875 when he became aware of the possibility of transmitting the human

This is the telegraph key that Samuel Morse used to send the first successful telegraph message on May 1, 1844. The intercity message read "What hath God wrought?" It was sent from a Supreme Court chamber in Washington, D.C., to Morse's assistant at the Mount Clair train depot in Baltimore, Maryland. The telegraph key is housed at the Smithsonian Institution's National Museum of American History in Washington, D.C.

voice directly across telegraph lines. On March 10, 1876, Bell made the first phone call to his assistant in the next room.

With the support of his wealthy father-in-law, Bell set up the Bell Telephone Company in 1877. Before the telephone could become available to everyone in the country, the invention had to be improved and a structure of cables and central telephone exchanges put into place. Only 230 telephones were installed in July 1877. A decade later, there were 170,000 telephones in the United States. By the time of Bell's death in 1922, the number had multiplied to over 9 million.

In the early years of the telephone, every call was transmitted to a central exchange. Female telephone operators would connect callers to the parties they wanted to reach. Long-distance

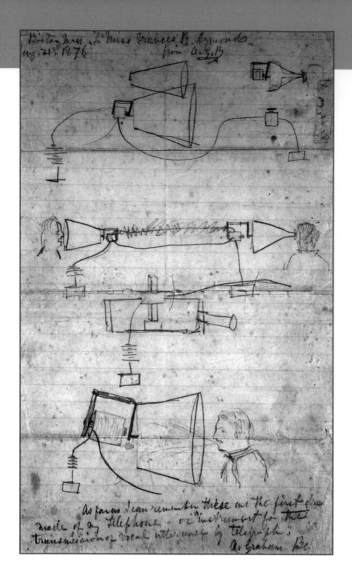

This is Alexander Graham Bell's design sketch of the telephone from around 1876. It bears a note in Bell's handwriting that reads, "As far as I can remember these are the first drawings made of my telephone—or 'instrument for the transmission of vocal utterances by telegraph.'" In Bell's first telephone call, made on March 10, 1876, to his assistant in another room, he said, "Mr. Watson, come here, I want to see you." Within hours of the time that Bell submitted the patent for his telephone, an inventor named Elisha Gray submitted a patent for a similar device. Fortunately for Bell, his patent was approved first.

telephone service began in 1884 with the construction of lines between Boston and New York. The telephone competed directly with the telegraph and eventually replaced it.

Edison and Electricity

Samuel Morse's telegraph inspired a teenage telegraph operator named Thomas Alva Edison to experiment with telegraph equipment and laboratory chemicals. After spending a few years drifting from one job to another, he decided to settle down and become an inventor. In 1869, at the age of twenty-two, Edison filed for his first patent, a vote recording device. Not long afterward, he set up his first laboratory in Newark, New Jersey.

During his lifetime, Edison received a record 1,093 patents. He was proudest of the phonograph, patented in 1877. According to biographer Paul Israel in *Edison: A Life of Invention*, Edison once told a reporter, "This is my baby and I expect it to grow up to be a big feller and support me in my old age." Today, people remember Edison best for perfecting the incandescent lightbulb, successfully tested in 1879. But Edison's most important achievement was his introduction of the electrical system in the United States.

In 1882, Edison supervised construction of the first electric light and power system in New York City. Six steam engines drove six jumbo generators, providing electricity to supply 8,000 Edison lamps. Similar power stations cropped up in cities and towns across the country. The Edison Electric Light Company managed the system, and companies such as the Edison Machine Works and the Edison Electric Tube Company provided the components.

But competition soon arrived. Edison based his power stations on low-voltage direct current (DC) electricity. DC could run through lines only for a short distance before starting to lose power. Expensive power stations had to be built about every 2 miles (3.2 km), an impracticality in rural areas. In 1888, Nikola Tesla, who had briefly worked in Edison's lab, devised a high-voltage alternating current (AC) system of power. AC was stronger and more efficient than DC, and it could travel long distances before starting to lose power. The inventor and industrialist George Westinghouse adopted AC electricity in a lighting system rivaling Edison's system.

The "war of the currents" followed, as Edison and Westinghouse both pitched their systems to the public. In 1893, the World's Columbian Exposition in Chicago used the AC

EDISON'S INVENTION OF THE KINETO-PHONOGRAPH.

In the year 1887, the idea occurred to me that it was possible to devise an instrument which should do for the eye what the phonograph does for the ear, and that by a combination of the two, all motion and sound could be recorded and reproduced simultaneously. This idea, the germ of which came from the little toy called the Zoetrope, and the work of Muybridge, Marié, and others has now been accomplished, so that every change of facial expression can be recorded and reproduced life size. The Kinetoscope is only a small model illustrating the present stage of progress but with each succeeding month new possibilities are brought into view. I believe that in coming years by my own work and that of Dickson, Muybridge Marié and others who will doubtless enter the field, that grand opera can be given at the Metropolitan Opera House at New York without any material change from the original, and with artists and musicians long since dead. The following article which gives an able and reliable account of the invention has my entire endorsation. The authors are peculiarly well qualified for their task from a literary standpoint and the exceptional opportunities which Mr Dickson has had in the fruition of the work.

Thomas A Edison

This note, written by Thomas Edison, prefaced an article entitled "Edison's Invention of the Kineto-Phonograph" by Antonia and W. K. L. Dickson in the June 1894 edition of *The Century*. Edison was very proud of this invention, which is a motion-picture camera. The invention marked the beginning of the motion picture industry. The first copyrighted motion picture showed one of Edison's employees pretending to sneeze.

lighting system. It was such a success that Westinghouse gained support to open the first large-scale AC power plant on Niagara Falls. The power plant was completed in 1896. AC power had been proven a better system than DC. Today's electrical systems depend on AC electricity.

A New Age of Scientific Research

In 1830, the United States government awarded its first grant for scientific research to the Franklin Institute to investigate why many steamboats malfunctioned or exploded. As America grew increasingly industrialized, each scientific and industrial advance opened opportunities for further research and development. The introduction of electricity led to the development of electric streetcars. New electric devices changed people's everyday lives. Scientists discovered a variety of uses and products of the new fuel, petroleum.

Thomas Edison pioneered the first American industrial research laboratory in Menlo Park, New Jersey. He aimed to "produce a minor invention every ten days and a big thing every six months or so," as quoted in Paul Israel's *Edison: A Life of Invention*. Teams of specialized scientists and engineers in a laboratory could produce more complex inventions than a single inventor working alone. As single companies came to dominate entire industries, they could afford to establish private research labs. By the beginning of the twentieth century, corporations such as Goodyear, General Motors, and Eastman Kodak had all set up research labs.

CHAPTER 4

LIFE AND WORK IN INDUSTRIAL AMERICA

When Samuel Slater and Francis Cabot Lowell opened their first factories, they had difficulties hiring and keeping workers. Many Americans considered factory work degrading. They believed that working by a time clock, under constant supervision, diminished their freedom. Slater employed children as well as adults in his mills. The use of child labor continued throughout the nineteenth century.

Lowell attracted young women to his factories by emphasizing the quality of the living and working conditions. But even in Lowell's model factories, workers voiced complaints. In 1845, a group of Lowell workers published "Factory Tracts" criticizing the Lowell system. A girl who gave only the name Amelia wrote of Lowell's "tyrannous and oppressive rules." She pointed out that a worker "finds herself compelled to remain for the space of twelve months in the very place she then occupies, however reasonable and just cause of complaint might be hers, or however strong the wish for dismission; thus, in fact, constituting herself a slave." Amelia also objected to crowded conditions, low pay, and long hours.

Throughout the nineteenth century, millions of immigrants poured into the United States. The rapid increase in the population contributed to economic growth and further spurred the Industrial Revolution. This engraving portrays German immigrants onboard a ship passing the Statue of Liberty as it arrives in New York City. It was published in *Frank Leslie's Illustrated Newspaper* on July 2, 1887.

The population of the United States rose dramatically through the nineteenth century. Factory owners no longer had problems finding willing workers. Some people were desperate enough to accept low wages and even the most wretched factory conditions without complaining. The typical worker earned less than a dollar a day in 1860, which would be about $22 today.

Working conditions deteriorated as industrialism became widespread. Besides requiring long hours of repetitive labor, factory work endangered the health of many workers. Workers were often subjected to hazardous fumes in unventilated areas.

A tired or careless worker could easily lose an eye or a limb or even die while working with machinery.

As the United States became an industrial power, immigrants from Europe began arriving in search of new opportunities. Because of the shortage of labor in early industrial America, manufacturers frequently encouraged immigration. Before the Civil War, the largest numbers came from Germany and Ireland. A wave of Scandinavian immigrants arrived after 1870, and millions immigrated from eastern Europe and Mediterranean countries beginning in the 1880s. A majority of the newcomers stayed in New York or moved to other large cities.

Some immigrants, such as many early Germans, were skilled craftsmen and helped propel the Industrial Revolution. Others arrived with few skills and took any job they could find. They provided a cheap source of industrial labor. Irishmen often worked in construction, especially for the railroad. Italians worked in the clothing industries. Women from all ethnic groups took positions in textile mills and other factories.

European immigrants and rural Americans flocked to urban areas in search of jobs. Cities grew rapidly during the nineteenth century. The new American city had impressive skyscrapers, strong new bridges, and wide streets lit by streetlamps. Many poor workers lived in slums, however, crowded into unhealthy tenement buildings.

The Labor Movement

In 1824, a cotton mill in Pawtucket, Rhode Island, erupted into flames, apparently caused by arson and widely believed to have been the work of disgruntled workers. The mill owners had recently demanded an increase of work hours at lower wages. Soon after the fire, the owners and workers reached a compromise.

Many industrial workers rebelled against poor working conditions in nineteenth-century industrial America. Yet few took the extreme step of destroying factories or equipment. Workers began joining together to form trade unions. They hoped that factory owners would take notice of their complaints if an entire group of workers spoke with the same voice. By acting together, workers could threaten to go on strike to force their demands. Even in Lowell, women went on strike during the 1830s and formed the Lowell Female Labor Reform Association in 1845.

Employers often reacted by firing union members and putting their names on blacklists. Factory managers shared these lists and refused to hire people involved in unions. Some businesses even took the unions to court. In 1835, the New York Supreme Court declared unions and strikes illegal after a tailors' union went on strike to protest wage reductions. Union supporters posted coffin-shaped handbills declaring, "The Rich Against the Poor! . . . Go! Every Freeman, every Workingman, and hear the melancholy sound of the earth on the Coffin of Equality. Let the Court Room, the City-hall—yea, the whole Park, be filled with mourners!" The park outside New York's city hall was packed with 27,000 people, demonstrating their support for organized labor.

After the Civil War, more people worked in huge factories with thousands of employees. Union membership soared and labor unions became a powerful force. Many union members also belonged to organizations that advocated political and social change as well as reform. Socialists and Communists, for example, believed that all property and political power should be shared among the people. Many poor workers, especially

The Knights of Labor wanted to create one big labor union consisting of all workers, regardless of race, sex, national origin, or skill level. Published in 1885, this broadside outlined the Knights of Labor's position on the labor issues of the day. Among its demands was the establishment of bureaus of labor standards; the adoption of safety measures for mining, factory, and construction workers; the establishment of a graduated income tax in which the poor paid less than the wealthy; an eight-hour work day; and equal pay for both sexes for equal work. Refer to page 55 for a partial transcription.

immigrants, hoped that the spread of these ideologies would bring them better lives.

Railroad workers started unionizing during the 1860s, forming the powerful "railway brotherhoods." The Knights of Labor, which supported the formation of a "cooperative commonwealth," was founded in 1869 and grew steadily through the 1870s. Unlike some unions, the Knights of Labor welcomed women, immigrants, and African Americans.

During the railroad strikes of 1877, the first widespread strikes in American history, the government intervened on the side of business. Over a hundred people died in skirmishes between military troops and crowds of demonstrators. The strikers were defeated, but the event brought renewed fervor to the labor movement.

On May 1, 1886, 350,000 workers across the country participated in a strike supporting an eight-hour workday. Two days later, police and workers clashed at the McCormick Reaper Works in Chicago, resulting in the deaths of at least two workers. On May 4, an unknown person threw a bomb into a rioting crowd at nearby Haymarket Square, killing seven policemen. The government and press blamed labor activists and anarchists for the incident. Eight anarchists were charged and convicted of conspiracy to commit murder, despite a lack of evidence.

The Knights of Labor gradually declined, and the American Federation of Labor (AFL) was formed in 1886. The AFL concentrated on concrete goals and collective bargaining rather than radical political and social change. In 1892, the president and founder Samuel Gompers was reluctant to endorse a candidate for president. As he wrote in the *North American Review*, the AFL was "not in harmony either with the existing or projected political parties." Regardless of election results, he wrote, "the American Federation of Labor will still be found plodding along, doing noble battle in the struggle for the uplifting of the toiling masses."

But periodic workers' strikes continued, sometimes ending in violence. In 1892, the workers at the Carnegie Steel Company in Homestead, Pennsylvania, went on strike. Employees worked twelve-hour days, seven days a week, and the manager had just announced that he was dissolving their union. The plant hired Pinkerton detectives (a group of private detectives notorious for their rough and often brutal methods) and called on the state governor to send in militia troops. The strikers were eventually defeated. In 1894, a strike by Pullman railway workers was similarly put down by railway management, state militias, and the U.S. Army. Tensions between big business and labor, with the government occasionally stepping in on the side of business, continued into the twentieth century.

Robber Barons and the Age of Big Business

The labor movement was opposed by large and powerful corporations. During the last decades of the nineteenth century, many small factories merged or were bought out to form larger companies. In some cases, a single corporation came to control an entire industry. A few industrialists helped build up these empires and became fabulously wealthy. They were called robber barons by some because of their perceived greed, foul play, and wholesale disregard for the welfare of their workers.

One of the greatest rags-to-riches stories was that of Andrew Carnegie. A Scottish immigrant, Carnegie worked his way out of poverty, beginning in factories and becoming a railway superintendent by the age of twenty-four. In 1864, he learned of the Bessemer process of making steel. Carnegie invested in iron and steel companies, coming to dominate the industry at the time that America began constructing an infrastructure of railways, bridges, and buildings. He also bought up businesses related to steel production, such as beds of iron ore, coal fields, steamship lines, and railroads. At one point Carnegie's wealth was estimated at $400 million, a vast fortune for his day.

Many reformers claimed that individuals with such great wealth had more clout in government than the average worker and thus hurt the democratic system. Critics also argued that the robber barons exploited workers without giving anything back to society. Carnegie defended "the concentration of business,

At the height of his career, Andrew Carnegie dominated the United States steel industry and was the richest man in the world. Carnegie was ruthless in competing against his business rivals and in resisting the initiatives of labor unions. Despite his cut-throat business tactics, Carnegie had a strong sense of civic duty. He created seven charitable organizations in the United States, including the Carnegie Corporation of New York. Between 1881 and 1917, Carnegie spent $56 million to build more than 2,500 libraries throughout the world. Mathew B. Brady took this photograph sometime around 1890.

industrial and commercial, in the hands of a few," as he wrote in an 1889 article for the *North American Review*, calling it a natural result of industrialization. According to Carnegie, men such as himself earned their fortunes through hard work and natural skill. He believed, however, that the elite rich had a responsibility to use their money for the public good. Carnegie wrote that a rich man should endow "free libraries, parks, and means of recreation by which men are helped in body and mind; works of art, certain to give pleasure and improve the public taste; and public institutions of various kinds . . . Thus is the problem of rich and poor to be solved." Carnegie lived up to his words, donating about $350 million to charity in the last years of his life.

Fifty-first

N 190

Congress of the United States of America;

At the First Session,

Begun and held at the City of Washington on Monday, the *second* day of December, one thousand eight hundred and eighty-*nine*.

AN ACT

To protect trade and commerce against unlawful restraints and monopolies.

Be it enacted by the Senate and House of Representatives of the United States of America in Congress assembled,

Sec. 1. Every contract, combination in the form of trust or otherwise, or conspiracy in restraint of trade or commerce among the several States, or with foreign nations, is hereby declared to be illegal. Every person who shall make any such contract or engage in any such combination or conspiracy, shall be deemed guilty of a misdemeanor, and, on conviction thereof, shall be punished by fine not exceeding five thousand dollars, or by imprisonment not exceeding one year, or by both said punishments, in the discretion of the court.

Sec. 2. Every person who shall monopolize, or attempt to monopolize, or combine or conspire with any other person or persons, to monopolize any part of the trade or commerce among the several States, or with foreign nations, shall be deemed guilty of a misdemeanor, and, on conviction thereof, shall be punished by fine not exceeding five thousand dollars, or by imprisonment not exceeding one year, or by both said punishments, in the discretion of the court.

Sec. 3. Every contract, combination in form of trust or otherwise, or conspiracy, in restraint of trade or commerce in any Territory of the United States or of the District of Columbia, or in restraint of trade or commerce between any such Territory and another, or between any such Territory or Territories and any State or States or the District of Columbia, or with foreign nations, or between the District of Columbia and any State or States or foreign nations, is hereby declared illegal. Every person who shall make any such contract or engage in any such combination or conspiracy, shall be deemed guilty of a misdemeanor, and, on conviction thereof, shall be punished by fine not exceeding five thousand dollars, or by imprisonment not exceeding one year, or by both said punishments, in the discretion of the court.

Sec. 4. The several circuit courts of the United States are hereby

---

The Sherman Antitrust Act was passed in 1890 to prohibit monopolies and to prevent large companies from working together to restrain trade or fix prices. Many labor unions opposed the legislation because they feared it would one day be used against them, as it later was. Refer to page 56 for a partial transcription of the Sherman Antitrust Act.

A handful of other entrepreneurs earned fortunes and power through their business skills during the late nineteenth century. Cornelius Vanderbilt amassed a large fortune by investing in shipping and later expanding into railroads. Another railroad investor named Jay Gould is best remembered for attempting to buy up and control the entire U.S. gold market in 1869, causing a major financial panic. By 1890, Gould owned the Western Union Telegraph Company and about 13,000 miles (20,921 km) of western railroads. Financial wizard John Pierpont Morgan invested in businesses ranging from railroads to life insurance with his firm J. P. Morgan and Associates. Morgan organized the U.S. Steel Corporation in 1901, then the largest corporation in the world.

In 1862, John D. Rockefeller helped found a petroleum refining company that eventually became the Standard Oil Company. Standard Oil grew through buying up other companies and cutting deals with the railroads shipping its product. In 1882, the company formed the Standard Oil Trust, merging 90 percent of U.S. oil refineries into one company and allowing Rockefeller to become the world's first billionaire.

During the 1890s, the antitrust movement began to target the huge corporations known as trusts. These big businesses monopolized, or controlled, the production and distribution of certain goods, quashing all possibility of competition from other companies. Working conditions were often terrible in factories controlled by trusts, since workers did not have any means of opposing the powerful businesses. Congress passed the Sherman Antitrust Act in 1890, but reformers and the government would not begin to effectively challenge trusts until the twentieth century. One of the antitrust movement's first successes was the breakup of Standard Oil.

CHAPTER 5

IMPACT OF THE INDUSTRIAL REVOLUTION

At the turn of the twentieth century, a number of inventors and entrepreneurs were attempting to perfect the automobile. Before 1895, most motor vehicles moved no faster than a horse. Automotive technology improved, but cars were still luxury items, available only to the wealthy. The automobile did not become affordable to average Americans until Henry Ford entered the industry. Henry Ford had a natural understanding of mechanical devices. As a child, he took apart watches and reassembled them. As a young man, he worked in a machine shop, and he later made a name for himself building and driving race cars. In 1903, he founded Ford Motor Company. Ford personally headed the company, supported by a savvy entrepreneurial team.

Unlike other auto companies, Ford aimed to market the automobile to the masses. Ford Motor Company began producing the affordable Model T in 1908. According to Robert Lacey in *Ford: The Man and the Machine*, Ford explained his goals in a speech when he unveiled the Model T. "I will build a motor car for the great multitude . . . constructed of the best materials, by the best men to be hired, after the simplest designs that modern engineering can devise . . . so low in price that no man making a good salary will be unable to own one." In 1910, Ford Motor Company produced more than 30,000 cars; by 1916, the number had risen to over 700,000. The Model T's price fell as production cost decreased. Henry Ford had succeeded in creating a car for the average American.

In many ways, Ford Motor Company was the first modern industry. Ford revolutionized manufacturing when he realized the potential of the assembly line. Instead of having workers move around to work on automobile parts, Ford's precisely timed system brought parts to the worker. Parts moved on conveyor belts, down tilted slides, and overhead on pulleys. The assembly-line system had been fully put into place by 1913, greatly reducing the cost of production.

In 1914, Ford introduced the "five-dollar day," a forty hour workweek wage plan for his employees. Productivity increased and fewer workers quit their jobs or skipped work. More workers were able to afford automobiles.

A Changed World

In 1913, Woodrow Wilson became the twenty-eighth president of the United States. Wilson's inaugural address highlighted both the beneficial and the harmful legacies of the Industrial Revolution. He praised the country as "incomparably great in its material aspects, in its body of wealth, in the diversity and sweep of its energy, in the industries which have been conceived and built up

This September 1896 photo shows Henry Ford sitting in his first Ford automobile on Grand Boulevard, in Detroit, Michigan. Born on a farm near Dearborn, Michigan, Ford held several jobs—including apprentice in a machine shop, traction car operator, and engineer at Edison Illuminating Company—before he began manufacturing automobiles. Ford's innovations in manufacturing, most notably the assembly line and his reform of the labor week, dramatically increased productivity. They also allowed him to avoid having to deal with labor unrest, which he despised, for a while.

by the genius of individual men and the limitless enterprise of groups of men." Later in the speech, Wilson addressed the evils caused by big business:

We have squandered a great part of what we might have used, and have not stopped to conserve the exceeding bounty of nature, without which our genius for enterprise would have been worthless and impotent, scorning to be careful, shamefully prodigal as well as admirably efficient. We have been proud of our industrial achievements, but we have not hitherto stopped thoughtfully enough to count the human cost, the cost of lives snuffed out, of energies overtaxed and broken, the fearful physical and spiritual cost to the men and women and children upon whom the dead weight and burden of it all has fallen pitilessly the years through.

At the start of the Industrial Revolution, the United States had been a small country occupying the length of the East Coast. Most Americans were of British descent. By the time Wilson became president, the United States spanned from the East Coast to the West. A network of railways had provided the means of populating every corner of the country. Affordable manufactured goods made life easier for the average American. An increasingly multicultural population swelled with millions of immigrants. African Americans, freed from slavery during the Civil War, began taking industrial jobs. Women had started to become part of the workforce.

Much has changed since Wilson spoke to Americans about the human cost of industry and the value of conserving nature. Laws have outlawed child labor and shortened the workday. The Occupational Safety and Health Act (OSHA), passed in 1970, regulates workplace conditions.

Americans have become increasingly environmentally conscious. As urban industry grew after the Civil War, cities became polluted and unhealthy. Smoke from burning coal turned cities black and damaged people's lungs. Factories dumped industrial waste into waterways and heaped waste onto unused land. Cities disposed of raw sewage in rivers. Poor workers crowded into unsanitary tenement houses with inadequate sewers and garbage collection. Since then, the government has enacted environmental and zoning regulations. Many people, however,

This photograph shows automobile workers constructing a Model T engine on an assembly line in a Ford Motor Company factory around 1914. Ford's establishment of the assembly-line process led to the successful mass production of automobiles and revolutionized manufacturing throughout the world. In 1916, the Ford Motor Company sold more than 736,000 Model T automobiles.

believe that the United States should work harder to conserve natural resources and protect the environment.

Toward the Future

Technological development accelerated during the Industrial Revolution and continues to shape and change our world. In 1903, Wilbur and Orville Wright successfully built and tested the first airplane on the dunes of Kitty Hawk, North Carolina. The

This photograph captures the first flight of the Wright brothers on December 17, 1903, in Kitty Hawk, North Carolina. Wilbur Wright runs alongside the flying machine as his brother Orville, lying on the lower wing, controls it. The flight lasted twelve seconds and covered 120 feet (37 m).

brothers owned a bicycle shop and experimented with manned flight in their spare time. The U.S. military tested and adopted a "Wright flyer" in 1909 and air-mail service began in 1918. Charles Lindbergh became a national hero in 1927 when he became the first person to fly a plane solo across the Atlantic Ocean.

During World War II (1939–1945), physicists in both Germany and the United States conducted experiments in nuclear energy. The world saw the devastating results of their research in 1945 when the United States dropped nuclear bombs on the Japanese cities of Hiroshima and Nagasaki. After the war, scientists turned to nuclear energy as a new source of power. The first nuclear power plants opened in the 1950s.

The twentieth century has seen incredible advances in science and medicine. Modern chemistry has transformed many aspects of our daily lives, from household products and pharmaceuticals to industrial compounds used to manufacture plastics and other synthetics. Vaccinations and antibiotics have helped conquer deadly diseases that were once considered incurable. Doctors performed the first successful heart transplant in 1967 and introduced the first fully implantable artificial heart in 2001. Scientists have successfully cloned animals and manipulated deoxyribonucleic acid (DNA), the basic building block of life, to produce bio-engineered plants and animals.

In 1895, the Italian inventor Guglielmo Marconi successfully sent and received the first long-distance radio transmissions, marking the next stage in the communications revolution. Radios became common in American households in the late 1920s. Television took hold in the late 1940s and early 1950s. The most recent development has been the rise of the Internet in the 1990s. It allows computer users easy access to a wealth of information and instant electronic communication.

Today, doctors are working to find a cure for AIDS. Some scientists hope to further develop solar and wind power to reduce America's dependence on fossil fuels. Computer technology continues to make new advances every year. The Industrial Revolution laid the foundation of a new age of innovation and progress, one that continues to the present day.

PRIMARY SOURCE TRANSCRIPTIONS

Page 13: Excerpt from Alexander Hamilton's *Report On Manufactures*– December 5, 1791

Transcription

It is now proper to proceed a step further, and to enumerate the principal circumstances from which it may be inferred that manufacturing establishments not only occasion a positive augmentation of the produce and revenue of the society, but that they contribute essentially to rendering them greater than they could possibly be without such establishments. These circumstances are:

1. The division of labor.
2. An extension of the use of machinery.
3. Additional employment to classes of the community not ordinarily engaged in the business.
4. The promoting of emigration from foreign countries.
5. The furnishing greater scope for the diversity of talents and dispositions, which discriminate men from each other.
6. The affording a more ample and various field for enterprise.
7. The creating, in some instances, a new, and securing, in all, a more certain and steady demand for the surplus produce of the soil.

Each of these circumstances has a considerable influence upon the total mass of industrious effort in a community; together, they add to it a degree of energy and effect which is not easily conceived . . .

The foregoing considerations seem sufficient to establish, as general propositions, that it is the interest of nations to diversify the industrious pursuits of the individuals who compose them; that the establishment of manufactures is calculated not only to increase the general stock of useful and productive labor, but even to improve the state of agriculture in particular,—certainly to advance the interests of these who are engaged in it . . .

Page 42: Excerpt from Preamble and Declarations of Principles of the Knights of Labor of America

Transcription

The alarming development and aggressiveness of great capitalists and corporations, unless checked, will inevitably lead to the pauperization and hopeless degradation of the toiling masses.

It is imperative, if we desire to enjoy the full blessings of life, that a check be placed upon unjust accumulation, and the power for evil of aggregated wealth.

This much-desired object can be accomplished only by the united efforts of those who obey the divine injunction, "In the sweat of thy face shalt thou eat bread."

Therefore we have formed the Order of the Knights of Labor, for the purpose of organizing and directing the power of the industrial masses, not as a political party, for it is more—in it are crystalized sentiments and measures for the benefit of the whole people, but it should be borne in mind, when exercising the right of suffrage, that most of the objects herein set forth can only be obtained through legislation, and that it is the duty of all to assist in nominating and supporting with their votes only such candidates as will pledge their support to these measures, regardless of party. But no one shall, however, be compelled to vote with the majority, and calling upon all who believe in securing the greatest good to the greatest number, to join and assist us, we declare to the world the our aims are:

1. To make industrial and moral worth, not wealth, the true standard of individual and national greatness.
2. To secure to the worker the full enjoyment of the wealth they create, sufficient leisure in which to develop their intellectual, moral and social faculties; all of the benefits, recreation and pleasures of association; in a word, to enable them to share in the gains and honors of advancing civilization.

In order to secure these results we demand of the State:

3. The establishment of bureaus of labor statistics, that we may arrive at a correct knowledge of the educational, moral, and financial condition of the laboring masses.
4. That the public lands, the heritage of the people, be reserved for actual settlers; not another acre for railroads or speculators, and that all lands now held for speculative purposes be taxed at their full value. . .

And so demand at the hands of Congress:

14. The establishment of a national monetary system, in which a circulating medium in necessary quantity shall issue direct to the people, without the intervention of banks; that all the national issue shall be full legal tender in payment of all debts, public and private; and that the government shall not guarantee or recognize any private banks, or create any banking corporations.
15. That interest-bearing bonds, bills of credit, or notes shall never be issued by the government, but that, when need arises, the emergency shall be met by issue of legal tender, non-interest-bearing money.
16. That the importation of foreign labor under contract be prohibited.

Page 46: Excerpt from the Sherman Antitrust Act (1890)

Transcription

Section 1. Trusts, etc., in restraint of trade illegal; penalty

Every contract, combination in the form of trust or otherwise, or conspiracy, in restraint of trade or commerce among the several States, or with foreign nations, is declared to be illegal. Every person who shall make any contract or engage in any combination or conspiracy hereby declared to be illegal shall be deemed guilty of a felony, and, on conviction thereof, shall be punished by fine not exceeding $10,000,000 if a corporation, or, if any other person, $350,000, or by imprisonment not exceeding three years, or by both said punishments, in the discretion of the court.

Section 2. Monopolizing trade a felony; penalty

Every person who shall monopolize, or attempt to monopolize, or combine or conspire with any other person or persons, to monopolize any part of the trade or commerce among the several States, or with foreign nations, shall be deemed guilty of a felony, and, on conviction thereof, shall be punished by fine not exceeding $10,000,000 if a corporation, or, if any other person, $350,000, or by imprisonment not exceeding three years, or by both said punishments, in the discretion of the court.

# GLOSSARY

acoustics   The science of sound.

anarchist   One who rebels against government, authority, or established order.

antibiotic   A chemical substance derived from mold, bacteria, or other organisms that destroys other microorganisms.

apprenticeship   The period of time in which a young man or woman learns an art or trade from a skilled worker.

artisan   A skilled worker or craftsman.

card   To cleanse, disentangle, and collect wool or cotton fibers before spinning.

charter   To establish and define a corporation.

clout   Influence, especially in political matters.

collective bargaining   Negotiations between employers and a group of organized workers such as a union.

commodity   Article in trade or commerce.

component   A part that forms or functions as part of a larger system.

cottage industry   Nonfactory production of goods, usually carried on at home by family members using their own equipment.

electromagnetism   Magnetism generated by a current of electricity.

entrepreneur   Someone who organizes and manages a business or enterprise and takes the risk for it.

flying shuttle   An improvement to weaving looms that increased a weaver's speed.

harrow   A cultivating machine with spikes, spring teeth, or discs that smooths the soil in fields.

immigration   The process of leaving one country to settle in another.

incandescent   Emitting light through heating by an electric current.

infrastructure   The basic facilities, services, and institutions needed for the functioning of a community or society.

mill A building with machinery for grinding grain into flour, or, more generally, a building containing machinery for manufacturing.

musket A type of old-fashioned firearm.

paddle wheel A large wheel fitted with paddles that turns in the water.

pharmaceutical A medicinal drug.

phonograph An early record player.

Pinkerton detectives Detectives belonging to the elite agency formed by Alan Pinkerton in 1852, known for their extremely effective and sometimes brutal methods.

ratify To formally approve.

revolver A pistol with a revolving cylinder that holds six bullets.

scythe A long, curved blade set at an angle onto a handle, used for mowing.

sickle A crescent-shaped blade set onto a short handle.

smelt To melt or fuse metal, often with the purpose of separation or purification.

synthetic A product of a chemical process (as opposed to a naturally occurring substance).

tenement An apartment house, often one occupied by poor families and having minimum standards of facilities and maintenance.

time clock A clock that monitors employees' starting and quitting times.

transcontinental Extending across a continent.

vaccination Administration of a preparation that will increase immunity to a specific disease.

yeoman A person who cultivates a small farm.

FOR MORE INFORMATION

Web Sites

Due to the changing nature of Internet links, the Rosen Publishing Group, Inc., has developed an online list of Web sites related to the subject of this book. This site is updated regularly. Please use this link to access the list:

http://www.rosenlinks.com/psah/inra

FOR FURTHER READING

Franck, Irene, and David M. Brownstone. *Manufacturers and Miners.* New York: Facts on File, 1988.

Josephson, Judith Pinkerton. *Mother Jones: Fierce Fighter for Workers' Rights.* Minneapolis, MN: Lerner Publications Company, 1997.

Lavine, Sigmund A. *Famous Industrialists.* New York: Dodd, Mead and Company, 1961.

Lomask, Milton. *Great Lives: Invention and Technology.* New York: Atheneum Books for Young Readers, 1991.

Stein, R. Conrad. *The Transcontinental Railroad in American History.* Springfield, NJ: Enslow Publishers, Inc., 1997.

Travers, Bridget, ed. *World of Invention.* Detroit, MI: Gale Research Inc., 1994.

# BIBLIOGRAPHY

Bender, Thomas. *Toward an Urban Vision: Ideas and Institutions in Nineteenth Century America.* Baltimore, MD: Johns Hopkins University Press, 1982.

Bourne, Russell. *Invention in America.* Golden, CO: Fulcrum Publishing, 1996.

Brier, Stephen, ed., et al. *Who Built America? Volume 2: 1877 to the Present.* New York: Worth Publishers, 2000.

Dudley, William, ed. *The Industrial Revolution: Opposing Viewpoints.* San Diego, CA: Greenhaven Press, Inc., 1998.

Hendrick, Burton J. *The Age of Big Business.* New Haven, CT: Yale University Press, 1919.

Hindle, Brooke, and Steven Lubar. *Engines of Change: The American Industrial Revolution 1790–1860.* Washington, DC: Smithsonian Institution Press, 1986.

Israel, Paul. *Edison: A Life of Invention.* New York: John Wiley and Sons, Inc., 1998.

Koch, Adrienne, and William Peden, eds. *The Life and Selected Writings of Thomas Jefferson.* New York: Random House, 1993.

Licht, Walter. *Industrializing America: The Nineteenth Century.* Baltimore, MD: The Johns Hopkins University Press, 1995.

Marcus, Alan I., and Howard P. Segal. *Technology in America: A Brief History.* New York: Harcourt Brace Jovanovich, 1989.

Murolo, Priscilla, and A. B. Chitty. *From the Folks Who Brought You the Weekend: A Short, Illustrated History of Labor in the United States.* New York: The New Press, 2001.

Orth, Samuel P. *The Armies of Labor.* New Haven, CT: Yale University Press, 1919.

Philip, Cynthia Owen. *Robert Fulton: A Biography.* New York: Franklin Watts, 1985.

Purcell, L. Edward. *Immigration.* Phoenix, AZ: The Oryx Press, 1995.

Pursell, Carroll. *The Machine in America: A Social History of Technology.* Baltimore, MD: The Johns Hopkins University Press, 1995.

Pursell, Carroll, ed. *Technology in America: A History of Individuals and Ideas.* Cambridge, MA: MIT Press, 1989.

Stalcup, Brenda, ed. *The Industrial Revolution.* San Diego, CA: Greenhaven Press, 2002.

Stearn, Gerald Emanuel, ed. *Gompers.* Englewood Cliffs, NJ: Prentice-Hall, Inc., 1971.

Thompson, Holland. *The Age of Invention.* New Haven, CT: Yale University Press, 1921.

Ware, Norman. *The Industrial Worker, 1840–1860: The Reaction of American Industrial Society to the Advance of the Industrial Revolution.* Chicago, IL: Ivan R. Dee, 1990.

PRIMARY SOURCE IMAGE LIST

Page 11: James Watt's first steam engine, created in 1763. Housed in the Science Museum in London, England.

Page 13: Page from *Report on Manufactures,* written by Alexander Hamilton in 1791. Housed in the Manuscript Division of the Library of Congress in Washington, D.C.

Page 15: Undated portrait of Samuel Slater, engraving. Artist unknown.

Page 16: American School painting portraying the first cotton mill in the United States. Oil on canvas, circa 1790. Housed at the Smithsonian Institution in Washington, D.C.

Page 18: Eli Whitney's patent for the cotton gin, 1794. Housed at the U.S. National Archives and Records Administration in Washington, D.C.

Page 18 (inset): Undated portrait of Eli Whitney. Artist unknown

Page 21: *Reaper at Work,* engraving by Burgess and Key, circa 1851.

Page 23: Time Table of the Lowell Mills, 1853. Housed at the American Textile History Museum in North Andover, Massachusetts.

Page 25: *First Trip of Fulton's Steamboat to Albany*, etching, circa 1807, by Samuel Hollyer. Housed at the Library of Congress Prints and Photographs Division in Washington, D.C.

Page 26: *Across the Continent,* hand-colored engraving, published in *Frank Leslie's Illustrated Newspaper* in 1878.

Page 29: *America,* painting by Joseph Nash, 1954. Housed at the British Library.

Page 31: Stereograph of oil derricks in Titusville, Pennsylvania, taken between 1860 and 1910. Part of the Robert Dennis Collection of Stereoscopic Views, photography collection, Miriam & Ira D. Wallach division of Art, Prints & Photographs, the New York Public Library.

Page 33: Samuel Morse's telegraph key used to send the first telegraph message. Housed at the National Museum of American History in Washington, D.C.

Page 34: Design sketch of the telephone by Alexander Graham Bell, 1876. Housed at the Library of Congress Manuscript Division in Washington, D.C.

Page 36: Thomas Edison's introduction to the article "Edison's Invention of the Kineto-Phonograph," published in *The Century* in 1894.

Page 39: Engraving portraying the arrival of German immigrants to New York City. Published in *Frank Leslie's Illustrated Newspaper* on July 2, 1887. Housed in the Library of Congress Prints and Photographs Division in Washington, D.C.

Page 42: Preamble and Declaration of Principles of the Knights of Labor of America. Published in the Journal of United Labor in 1885. Housed at the Library of Congress in Washington, D.C.

Page 45: Photograph of Andrew Carnegie, circa 1890, taken by Mathew B. Brady. Housed at the Library of Congress in Washington, D.C.

Page 46: Page from the Sherman Antitrust Act of 1890. Housed at the National Archives in Washington, D.C.

Page 50: Photograph of Henry Ford with his first automobile. Taken in September 1896.

Page 51: Circa 1914 photograph of assembly-line workers at a Ford Motor Company factory.

Page 53: Photograph of Wright brothers' first flight in Kitty Hawk, North Carolina, on December 17, 1903. Housed at the Library of Congress Prints and Photographs Division in Washington, D.C.

INDEX

About the Author

Corona Brezina is a freelance writer who lives in Chicago, Illinois.

Photo Credits

Cover, p. 1 © Corbis; pp. 9, 20, 52 Hulton Archive/Getty Images; pp. 11, 15, 50 © Bettmann/Corbis; pp. 13, 34 Library of Congress, Manuscript Division; p. 16 Smithsonian Institution, Washington DC/Bridgeman Art Library; pp. 18 (left), 46 http://www.ourdocuments.gov; p. 18 (right) New Haven Colony Historical Society p. 23 American Textile History Museum; pp. 25, 39, 45, 53 Library of Congress, Prints and Photographs Division; p. 26 courtesy of the Bancroft Library, University of California, Berkeley; p. 29 The Stapleton Collection/Bridgeman Art Library; p. 31 Robert Dennis Collection of Stereoscopic Views, Photography Collection, Miriam and Ira D. Wallach Division of Art, Prints, and Photographs, New York Public Library Astor, Lenox, and Tilden Foundations; p. 33 © National Museum of American History, Smithsonian Institution; p. 36 © Cornell University Library; p. 42 Chicago Historical Society.

Designer: Nelson Sá; **Editor:** Wayne Anderson;
Photo Researcher: Peter Tomlinson